THE MARGINALS
by Kate Brennan

Published by Ignition Arts.

1st Ed. March 15, 2026

marginal:
(adj) situated at the edge of something
(n) a plant that grows in water adjacent to the edge of land

Laney does Art Abandonment (AA) throughout the play. Art Abandonment is a real art experiment where people around the world create art of all kinds and abandon it with kind notes for strangers to find.

Maybe you should try it.

Thank you, Tim Gallagher, Jessica DalCanton & MC3 for your commitment to evolving artists.

CHARACTERS

LANEY - new, expressive, can make people sneeze
D'NAY - student body president, used to dance, can move time forward or backward 3 seconds
HALE - 62 year old professor, erudite, good-humored, perpetually looks 17
VEN - has a heart of gold, looks like a different person every day
VEN2 - Ven on another day
VEN3 - Ven on another day
CRUX - a good friend, but distant, from a family of fly-ers, claims to hover 5 millimeters
FITZROW - goes with the flow, can zoom from one destination to another, but can never choose where
TRUNE - straightforward, D'Nay's second in command, can make people forget what they are about to say
GRAYNE - woke enough to need a nap, completes Kelton's sentences, can smell big emotions
KELTON - wears the other half of Grayne's friendship necklace, loves an idiom, can make people 20% sleepier
CHARTREUSE - a jaded unicorn, inherently artistic, can make everything...chartreuse

ENSEMBLE - rockstar singer(s)/movers for the Plantae Lingua sequence, also to play students throughout

NOTES ON THE PIECE

Ze, Zer, Zers are the pronouns of the play. All characters appear between the ages of 16-21. Characters and the actors who play them can be any race/identity/gender/orientation. When characters are first introduced in the text, it is poetic, not literal.

Top: Trune, D'Nay; Middle: Fitzrow, Laney, Crux; Grayne, D'Nay, Kelton, Bottom: Ven, Chartreuse; 📷: Lou Liguori

The Marginals premiered on April 10, 2025 at Montgomery County Community College's Blackbox at the Blue Bell Campus. It was directed by Tim Gallagher. The cast featured:

LANEY - Goose Rhoads
D'NAY - Gabrielle Boone
HALE - Makiya Smith
VEN - Myles Daniels
VEN2 - Dom Hernandez
VEN3 - Amy Reichling
CRUX - Ethan Peyton
FITZROW - Nick Decolli
TRUNE - Hannah Hang
GRAYNE - Hannah Redding-Gurczynski
KELTON - Belle Ragazzo
CHARTREUSE - Thomas Mayes

ENSEMBLE – Morgan Kelliehan, Haven Kortz
John Lebo, Leila Hadjali, Kayla Alderfer & Vic Bewley

Above: Ven, Laney, Hale 📷: Lou Liguori

PRODUCTION TEAM

Director: Tim Gallagher
Stage Manager: Bre Freeman
Assistant Director: Zaki Coleman
Assistant Director/ Dramaturg: Maeve Brennan
Set Designer: Nick Decolli
Properties Designer: Tommy Mayes
Costume Designer: Ally Cole
Lighting Designer: Maeve Brennan, Morgan Krause
Sound Designer: Nora Redmond
Puppet Designer: Gray Santino
Technical Director: Tim Gallagher
Assistant Technical Director: Xander Soboleski
Assistant Stage Manager: Leo Inzerillo
Consent Director: Gabrielle Boone
Choreography/Hair & Makeup Designer: Makiya Smith
Costumer Shop Manager: Seth Miller
Master Electrician: Vic Bewley
Asst. Puppet Designer: Steele Stevens, Ryan Hinderliter
Orchestrator/ Additional Music by: Norman Hocker
Production Management: Katherine Fritz
Graphic Designer: Gloria Young
Board Operators: Erik Butler, Morgan Krause
Crew: Dinia Hernandez, Grace Freeman-Bibbs, Ally Cole
Scenic Production: Ally Cole, Seth Miller, Morgan Krause, Maeve Brennan, Victoria Bewley, Nora Redmond, Amy Reichling, Ethan Peyton, Milo Morales, Hannah Redding -Gurczynski, John Lebo, Wyatt Lament, Elizabeth Kieser, Caleb Karlson, Leo Inzerillo, Dinia Hernandez, Grace Freeman-Bibbs, Dash Durning, Myles Daniels, Russel Cole, Jake Batchelder, Ryan Hinderliter, Steele Stevens, Gray Santino, Tommy Mayes, Nick Decolli, Makiya Smith

SCENE 1: Welcome Back, Losers

The auditorium at the School for the Marginally Magical. D'NAY takes the podium in front of the assembled student body. D'Nay is a firework that has been set off too many times. It is the first day of class.

D'NAY

The end of the world is upon us.

Climate change is irreversible, gun violence is ubiquitous, our leaders are corrupt and our representatives are for sale. Our oceans are polluted, our lands abused, our natural resources taken for granted and squandered like opportunity after opportunity to change our ways. There is plastic in our blood and there are microchips in our pockets. We are products of the quick fix, the fast food, the unnatural high, the self-medicated sedation, and we believe that more is more is more is more is more while nothing is ever is ever is ever enough.

Corporations are people, but people are robots. And the robots with all the money are robbing us blind and making us pay for the privilege to do so. Our planet is dying while we sip overpriced iced caramel macchiatos and big business is profiting while we subscribe and save to keep them in the black.

Our generation has the highest rates of depression and anxiety ever recorded, we have lost the ability to make eye contact, to make art, to make space, to communicate, to feel – feelings, empathy, community. Community is a word we use liberally but don't actually take the time, effort or focus to understand because it might mean we have to look at ourselves, our habits, our shortcomings, our wrongs, and change.

We stuff ourselves full of Sugar, Celebrity, and Questionable Content and then wonder why we feel Anxious, Inadequate and Alone. We are slaves to the Unending Scroll, disciples of Demagogues and lackeys to Likes. We are champions of a comparison culture that punishes us with every post and we are victims of the chaos we Ourselves create at every opportunity to do so.

Laney enters late.
There is minor hub bub "excuse me," "sorry" etc.

D'Nay sneezes.

'Scuse me. Our spines are degenerating like the Neanderthals we are becoming, and we respond to clicks like the Pavlovian dogs we are. We have a million online friends but no one to call in a crisis. We have a thousand followers but no one's got our back. We are Tired and Wired, Stretched and Depressed, Overcommitted and Undernourished. We are so woke we need a nap.

We are quick to cancel, slow to move and impossible to change.

I get up here every year hoping for a radical transformation, but we are so mired in self-loathing and enamored with self-deception, we continue to dig our own graves while we are killing ourselves to shovel the ever-loving dirt.

So, welcome to another year at the School for the Marginally Magical. Hope we can make this year different,

but it doesn't seem likely.

D'NAY begrudgingly takes a seat onstage.

Slow clap from scattered students.
HALE takes the podium.
Hale is a nonfiction library book in human form who perpetually looks 17.

HALE

Thank you, D'Nay, as always, for that uniquely bleak, albeit not inaccurate sentiment. Let's hear it for our student body president, D'Nay Johns.

Unenthusiastic clap.

D'NAY

Calling from seat

Only cause *literally* no one else wanted it.

HALE

Harsh but true, D'Nay. Harsh but true.

D'NAY

Literally. No one.

HALE

Thank you, D'Nay.

Welcome, everyone, particularly to our new students. As you can see, we are committed to freeing the opinionated, if often stark, perspectives of the student body, whatever your magical ability may be. Some final announcements before we adjourn: 1. You (SKIP 3 SECONDS) course schedules at the–

Hale eyes D'Nay. D'Nay shrugs like "What?!" (D'Nay in fact made time jump forward 3 seconds.)

(Clears throat) As *I was about to say*, 1. You can pick up your course schedules from the front office if you have not yet done so and 2. The new course "Maximize your Marginality" taught by Professor Jinks still has a few slots available if you find you have room in your schedule. And a friendly reminder to all students– new, old, even dare I say, student body representatives, (eyeing D'Nay) *please refrain from using your MAs during school hours unless explicitly instructed in class to do so.*

Thank you all and have a great year!

SCENE 2: Well that was...

The hallway before class. LANEY is a young octopus-cute, investigatory and unusual. CRUX is an understated diamond - cool, but created under pressure.

LANEY

Well that was

CRUX

boring?

LANEY

Informative. Now I feel even worse for being late. What did I miss? Were there performances? Dance numbers? Other speeches? We didn't have student government at my old school.

CRUX

No, there definitely weren't any dance numbers. There is literally nothing even vaguely *(can't find the word, gestures instead and makes a noise)* at this school.

LANEY

Well in any event that was

CRUX

Typical? Meaningless?

LANEY

Oh - I was gonna say, uh,

VEN enters.

Ven is a slap bracelet that changes colors with the wearer's mood – quick to jab but holds on tightly.

VEN

Rough? Painful? Depressing?

CRUX

Ven.

VEN

Crux.

CRUX

How was your summer?

VEN

Rough, painful, depressing. How was yours?

CRUX

Boring, typical, meaningless. This is Laney. Laney, Ven.

VEN

Laney.

LANEY

Ven.

Laney slips art abandonment into a locker, or drops it on a bench, the floor.

CRUX

What was that?

LANEY

Oh, nothing.

FITZROW zooms by as if traveling fluidly by hover board.

Fitzrow is an inflatable tube figure blowup from the 60s – wacky, lovable and hard to hold down.

VEN & CRUX

Fitzrow!

FITZROW

Ven!

LANEY

Catching up

Fitzrow?

FITZROW

Crux!

CRUX

This is Laney!

VEN

That's Fitzrow. Fitzrow can –

FITZROW

What up, Laney! Lataaaaaaah!

Fitzrow is gone.

VEN

See ya, dude! Fitzrow can –

CRUX

Not for us to say, Ven. Not for us to say.

VEN

Well, it's kind of– (noticing Crux's expression) Right. Sorry.

CRUX

Rule number one here at SMM: do not *out* another marge.

LANEY

Marge?

VEN

"Marginally Magical Person." Individual. Entity. You. Me. Crux. The lucky ones. The –

LANEY

Ah, I see.

CRUX

Okay okay we get it.

CRUX

So don't like divulge what someone else can do. It's rude.

VEN

But you can share *your MA* if you want.

LANEY

My –

VEN

You know, your MA, your *Magical Ability.*

CRUX

Pressuring others to divulge their MAs, also: not cool.

VEN

What?

CRUX

Oh please.

VEN

I wasn't doing anything of the sort. Besides, I'm an open book. I'm happy to share what I can do.

CRUX

Laney's not interested.

LANEY

I'm kinda interested.

VEN

See.

CRUX

Plenty of time for you to talk about yourself later, Ven. Right now, I have to get Laney to class. Ze's new. Obviously. I'm showing zer around.

VEN

Of course. Welcome, Laney, welcome. As you can see, we are vaguely disgruntled, moderately disillusioned, and completely average here. Congratulations on your enrollment. How are you feeling on your first day?

LANEY

Really considering

Uuuuh. Excited, nervous. A little overwhelmed. Grateful to Crux for being so generous with me–

VEN

Oh, wow. You really answered the question. I wasn't –I thought you would say something like "good" or "fine." Is your MA that you have to share all your feelings or something?

LANEY

Uh no.

CRUX

(to Ven for continuing to prod)

C'mon!

Chartreuse walks by.

Chartreuse is a jaded unicorn - colorful but completely pissed about it.

VEN

What up, Chartreuse!

CHARTRUESE

Don't talk to me.

Chartreuse is nearly gone.

VEN

Given the fact that people around here have the emotional range of like a doorknob, that was not an unreasonable question.

CHARTREUSE

without missing a step

I heard that Ven!

VEN

teasing Chartreuse

Omigod, is your MA that you can hear extremely well?

CHARTREUSE

You know it's not.

Chartreuse is gone.

VEN

So I guess you seem, uh, emotionally evolved in the greater context of here.

LANEY

I will take that as a compliment.

Noticing Hale off and clearly taken.

Who is *that*?

CRUX

Who?

LANEY

The uh, the one with the, uh -

(gestures to indicate something indicative of the individual playing Hale, perhaps great hair, glasses, or outfit)

CRUX

Hale?

VEN

Weren't you at assembly?

LANEY

I came in late.

VEN

Ah.

CRUX

Oh no.

LANEY

increasingly enamored

Hale, did you say?

VEN

Cute, right?

LANEY

back pedaling

Well, uh, I guess.

CRUX
chastising

Ven.

VEN
to Crux

What? Laney is new. We should introduce zer to everyone. (to Laney) You should totally ask Hale out.

LANEY

Oh, no. I wouldn't –

VEN
Calling

Hale!

LANEY

Omigod, don't.

CRUX
Knowingly

Seriously, don't.

HALE enters.

HALE

Vendyn. Cruxley.

CRUX

Hello.

VEN

Good to see you.

HALE

What discoveries did you make over summer recess?

CRUX

I conquered my fear of heights. My sister took me flying.

HALE

Well done.

VEN

to Laney

Crux's sister can fly. Like, in the air.

CRUX

Yeah, I think ze got it.

LANEY

Oh I thought we weren't supposed to out another Marge.

HALE

Still following that archaic rule, are we?

VEN

It's fine to talk about people with *real* magical powers.

CRUX

It's rude to out people who only have marginal abilities.

LANEY

Like us.

HALE

And why is that exactly? Shame? Embarrassment?

VEN

I'm not embarrassed. Like I told Laney here, I'm an open book. / I would happily –

CRUX

Some of us –

HALE

What do I always say? "Marginal" does not only mean insignificant. "It is in the margins–

VEN & CRUX

by rote

–that people take the notes."

HALE

And?

LANEY

Pipes in

And a marginal is a plant that grows in the water next to the land.

HALE

Precisely! A very unique and beautiful ability if I do say so. (to Laney) Hello, I don't believe we've met.

VEN

Oh, right. This is Laney. (suggestively) Ze was *interested* in meeting you.

LANEY

Oh, I –

HALE

Laney, you must be new.

LANEY

Hi. Hello. Yes. I am.

HALE

eyeing Ven

The joke never gets old I see.

A pleasure to meet you, Laney. I will be upfront with you and share, though you are under no obligation to do so, as Cruxley would indubitably state, that my MA is that I do not physically age beyond 17 years old. My mind continues to mature, naturally, but this "quintessence of dust" remains frozen in time.

LANEY

Oh, uh, then how old are you actually? Wait, I'm sorry– was that rude to ask.

HALE

Not at all, it's natural for young minds to be curious. We encourage that at SMM.

CRUX

Under zer breath

And here it comes…

HALE

I am 62 years of age and I am your biology and sexual education professor.

LANEY

Omigod.

HALE

Now, if you will head into the room, (*calling*) class, are you all ready to begin?

VEN

to Crux

I think Hale secretly loves tricking newbies.

HALE

Or perhaps it is you who delights in tricking "newbies," as you call them, Vendyn–, but one must take advantage of enjoying one's MA, don't you think, rather than live in shame of it?

Fitzrow overhears while zooming by.

FITZROW

Rock on, Professor Hale.

HALE

Rock on, Fitzrow.

Hale enters class with Ven & Crux. Laney trails behind.

FITZROW

Have a great first day, Laney!

LANEY

Omigod I almost hit on my sex ed professor.

FITZROW

Aw man, we've all been there.

LANEY

Have we though?

FITZROW

Once I left Professor Jinks in the sink overnight.

LANEY

You what?

FITZROW

Uh, I gotta get to Calc! *(frustrated by zooming in the wrong direction)* Come on!

Fitzrow is gone.

LANEY

I feel. I feel. I feel....so embarrassed.
(sigh) And that's okay.

Laney slips another AA into a locker, drops on floor, places on bench etc.

Here we go.

& heads into class.

SCENE 3: Participation is Fun

Students mill about an activity fair. The student government is one of several tables set up. Others may include Photography Club, Mathletes, Chess Club, The Yearbook, Improv Club or more apropos or funnier clubs. The Dance Club and all arts clubs are conspicuously empty. Throughout, the other tables are consistently better populated than the student government table. D'Nay persons a table with TRUNE, a computerized magnifying glass, unsuccessfully trying to recruit for student government.

D'NAY

calling to passing students

Change begins with you!

TRUNE

echoing unenthusiastically

Change begins with you.

D'NAY

The bees are dying.

TRUNE

The bees are dying.

D'NAY

Join student government.

TRUNE

Join student government.

Chartreuse passes by.

CHARTREUSE

Wild horses couldn't drag me.

D'Nay has flyers or folders or a banner or something that is definitely white.

D'NAY

C'mon, Chartreuse–

CHARTREUSE

Waste. Of. Time.

D'NAY

–use your powers for good.

CHARTREUSE

Left ya a little present.

When D'Nay pulls out the flyers or unrolls the banner it has turned from white to chartreuse (Chartreuse can turns things... you guessed it, chartreuse.)

D'NAY

Come on!

CHARTREUSE

Sashay Sashay, D'Nay, D'Nay. Go back to ballet, ballet. Student government doesn't look good on you.

D'NAY

Neither does lime green!

CHARTREUSE

Next time it'll be your pants.

Chartreuse exits.

D'NAY

I hate this color.

TRUNE

It really doesn't look good on anybody.

Grayne walks by, escorting a potted plant.
Grayne is super woke and offended by what you said.
The potted plant is, in fact, a professor.

TRUNE (cont.)

Hey Grayne, Professor.

D'NAY

Trying to recruit Grayne

Grayne, you are very – you have a distinct– you– I literally cannot think of what to say that would sound complimentary right now. Join student government. You can give speeches and people have to listen to you.

GRAYNE

(sniffs) Something around here stinks.

D'NAY

Grayne, you always say that.

GRAYNE

D'Nay, student government is not inclusive of me and my perspective.

D'NAY

That's because you won't be in it!

GRAYNE

It's because it is part of a hierarchical system that oppresses people and I don't feel represented.

D'NAY

That's because – omigod, I feel like I just had this conversation and I didn't even go back in time!

GRAYNE

See you later, Trune.

TRUNE

See you. *(Acknowledging the plant:)* Professor.

Grayne exits with Professor (plant).

D'NAY

Whatever. You pay taxes while corporations don't.

TRUNE

You pay taxes while corporations don't.

Turning to D'Nay

Wouldn't you rather just go back to dancing?

D'NAY glances wistfully towards the Dance Team booth, which is abandoned.

D'NAY

You know it's not *encouraged* and I kinda want my kids to have potable water so.

TRUNE

You don't have kids.

D'NAY

(about Trune) Give me strength.
(Calling to passersby) 25 million hectares of the Amazon have been lost to soybean growth.

TRUNE

25 million – what?

Laney wanders by and stops.

LANEY

What's a hectare?

D'NAY

A lot.
You're new.

TRUNE

Want to join student government?

LANEY

Uh, maybe. I – Don't you have to be elected, though?

TRUNE

Not here, you don't.

D'NAY

Wait. You're serious.

Laney shrugs. Why not?

D'NAY (cont.)

Hold up. Who are you? Ven?

LANEY

What?

D'NAY

Ven, come on.

LANEY

Ven? What are you –

D'NAY

Not missing a beat

Forget it. You're really new, huh.
Did someone put you up to this?

LANEY

No.

Trune's questions are quick-fire.

TRUNE

Wait. Is your MA that you have the ability to believably feign interest in things you don't care about?

LANEY

No.

TRUNE

Is it that you are obligated to say yes to everything people ask you?

LANEY

No.

TRUNE

Is it that you can make people believe things that aren't true?

LANEY

If I could do that, would I be at *this* school?

TRUNE

Touché.

D'NAY

And no one put you up to this? Not Ven, not Chartreuse, not Kelton?

LANEY

No. Really.

TRUNE

So then. You just say what you feel?

LANEY

Generally. Yes?

TRUNE

Wow. Why?

D'NAY

Well then, it's a pleasure to meet you.

TRUNE

Still hung up on Laney's behavior

Like anything you feel. You just *(express it)*

LANEY

I. do.

D'NAY

I'm D'Nay. This is Trune. We are student body president and –

TRUNE

–vice president, secretary, treasurer, representatives and whatever else student government is supposed to do.

LANEY

Where's the rest–?

TRUNE

No. We are all of those things. D'Nay is president and I'm the rest of the positions.

LANEY

Oh, I'm Laney. I just moved from the Boundary (back in time 3 seconds, repeated exactly:) I'm Laney. I just moved from the Boundary (again) I'm Laney. I just moved from the Boundary Terr-i-tor-ies—-Whoa. What just happened?

D'NAY

Nice. My MA is I can make time jump forward or backward 3 seconds.

LANEY

Wow. And you just did that. That's pretty amazing. I could see that coming in useful for like… tripping and when you have to get needles. But I tho—-(suddenly confused) I'm sorry. I just forgot what I was about to say.

TRUNE

I'm Trune. I can make you forget what you were about to say.

LANEY

Okay. Oh, that's interesting.
I – I thought. *(trying to recombobulate)* Just a sec.

TRUNE

Yeah, it'll only last for a few seconds.

D'NAY

Like all the changes we are capable of making.

TRUNE

So what's your party trick?

LANEY

My–? Oh, my MA? Ok, now I remember what I was going to – . Aren't you– . I'm sorry – someone told me that it wasn't uh, appropriate to talk about our MAs.

D'NAY

Lemme guess.

D'NAY & TRUNE

Crux.

D'NAY

That is because Cruxley can hover 3 millimeters above the ground and is embarrassed because I can make – *(makes time skip 3 seconds)*

LANEY

– because you can – wait. Did you just do it again?

D'NAY

Guilty.
90% of the hummingbird's natural habitat will be destroyed in 70 years. Does talking about a little trait you were born with seem important on a grand scale?

LANEY

Well, when you put it that way…

TRUNE

But really. Do you want to be on student government. You can be Treasurer. Or Secretary.

D'NAY

Honestly you can be Vice President if you want.

TRUNE

Hey.

Laney slips AA on the table.

D'NAY

What's that?

LANEY

Oh, it's this little. Project. I do. It's called Art Abandonment.

TRUNE

reading

"Be the change" Hey, this one's for you D'Nay. Cute.

LANEY

Have you heard of it?

D'NAY

Don't let anyone see you doing this.

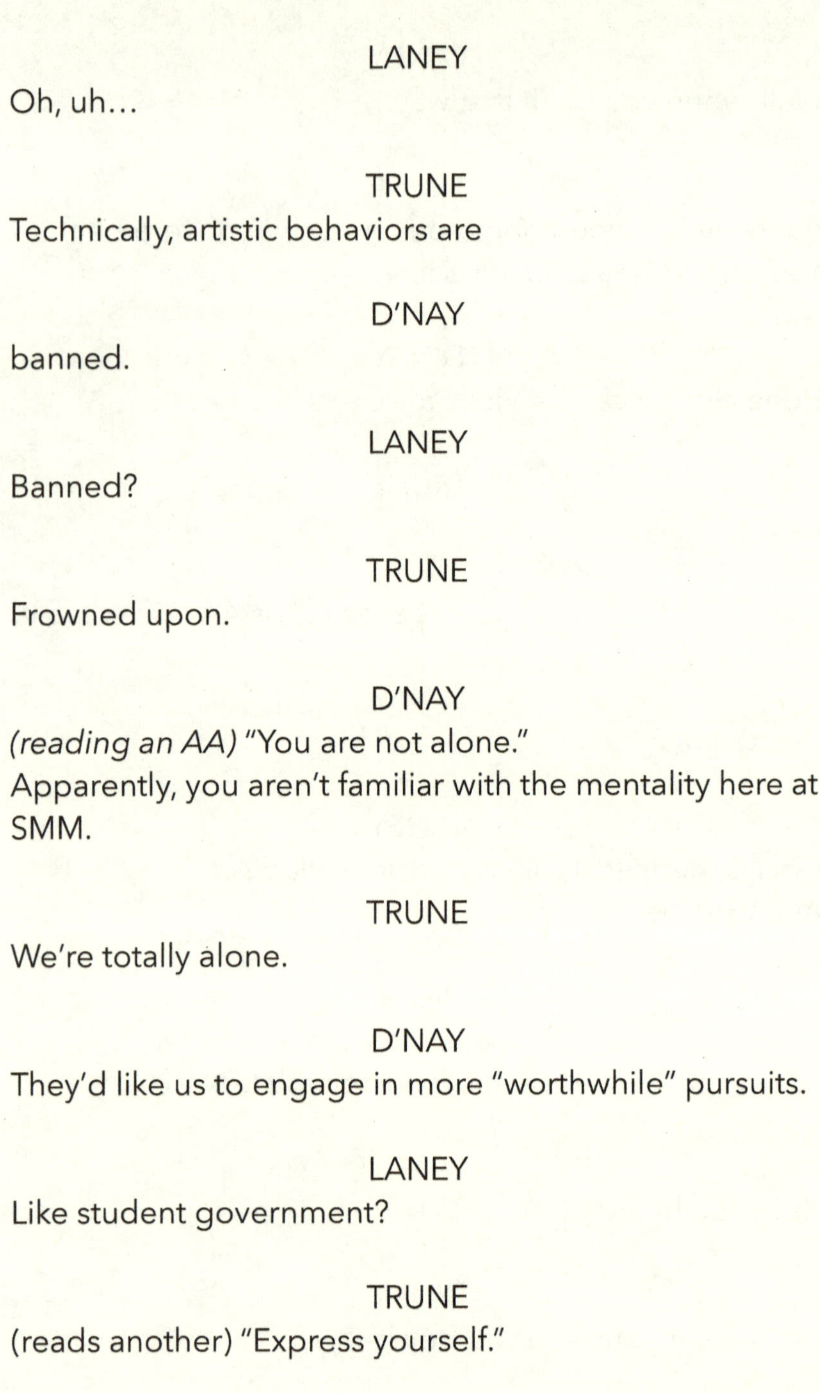

LANEY

Oh, uh…

TRUNE

Technically, artistic behaviors are

D'NAY

banned.

LANEY

Banned?

TRUNE

Frowned upon.

D'NAY

(reading an AA) "You are not alone."
Apparently, you aren't familiar with the mentality here at SMM.

TRUNE

We're totally alone.

D'NAY

They'd like us to engage in more "worthwhile" pursuits.

LANEY

Like student government?

TRUNE

(reads another) "Express yourself."

D'NAY

Try again.

LANEY

Actually, I think this one is for you, D'Nay.

Laney hands D'Nay an AA bookmark.
D'NAY takes it and reads.

D'NAY

"Be your own art."

D'Nay glances toward dance table.

TRUNE

Reading over D'Nay's shoulder

"Be your own art."

D'NAY

That's....

Fitzrow zooms by.

FITZROW

(to D'NAY)

Wicked speech, babe! Got you this. It's organic, vegan and sustainably made. *(Passes D'Nay something while zipping by - a smoothie, a trinket, a flower.)*

D'NAY

Thanks, babe. You make this uninhabitable world more habitable.

FITZROW

So do you babe, so do you!
Hey Trune, don't let the system get ya down!
What up, Laney! How was Bio?

LANEY

Should I join student government?

FITZROW

Truth to power!

FITZROW is gone.

LANEY

What does that mean?

D'NAY

It means

D'NAY & TRUNE

YES!

SCENE 4: The Plants Can Talk

The next day. Professor Jinks' "Maximize your Marginality" Class. Students (VEN2, GRAYNE, KELTON & D'NAY) are standing arms akimbo, palms splayed, with eyes closed in a Tai-Chi-esque meditative state. A potted plant (Professor Jinks) sits prominently at the front of the room. Ven2 is Ven but portrayed by an entirely different actor.

Laney rushes in.

LANEY

to Kelton

Is this "Maximize your Marginality?"

KELTON nods.

Kelton is a pin art mold and takes the impression of whoever is around.

LANEY

Thanks.

Laney is discombobulated.

VEN2

Psst. Laney. Over here.

Laney is surprised to be recognized, but slips next to Ven2.

LANEY

Um. Thanks. Sorry, have we *(met)*–

D'NAY opens an eye and spies Laney.

D'NAY

Hey, Lane. Took my suggestion, I see.

LANEY

Yeah, there was still room, so I just registered and –

GRAYNE is a blowfish, prickly at the slightest touch.

GRAYNE

trying to pay attention to something

SHHHHH - -

LANEY

Oh, sorry.

Laney is perplexed.
Why the shushing?

VEN2

to Grayne

Ze's new.

GRAYNE

Cry me a river. I'm trying to pay attention over here.

LANEY

Um. I'm sorry. What exactly –

KELTON & GRAYNE

SHHHHHH!

GRAYNE

What is that smell?

LANEY

Is something...?

VEN2

Raising hand politely, addressing the plant

'Scuse me, Professor.

Students all relax and open their eyes to look at Ven2 who has been called upon by the plant professor. Ven2 is now speaking to Professor Jinks who, just to reinforce, is an actual, literal potted plant.

There's a student talking to a plant. You read that right.

VEN2

addressing plant

Laney is not from here and I –

LANEY

Who are you *(talking to)* –

GRAYNE

Man, you are rude and *(recognizing smell is coming from Laney's general direction)* Oh.

LANEY

What?

VEN2

Unruffled

Laney is from the Boundary Territories where I'm guessing they don't have Plantae Lingua.

LANEY

Plantae –?

KELTON

What, did you grow up – in a barn?

Is it though?

GRAYNE

–under a rock?
"Rock" is better./ They don't have -

LANEY

trying to say the words she just heard

We don't have Plllll– (Plantae Lingua)

VEN2

To professor

Do you mind if I take a second to explain?

Ven2 receives an answer from the professor. Maybe you find a way to make the professor's response known a la the adults in the Peanuts or through the air or in lighting shifts.

Thank you, Professor.

Ven2 turns to Laney.

Okay.

Tries to explain.

It's sort of hard to explain.

D'NAY

Professor Jinks turns into a plant on every new moon.

LANEY

I'm sorry, what?

VEN2

You know how there are eight stages to the moon: new Moon, waxing crescent, first quarter, waxing gibbous, full Moon, waning gibbous, third quarter and waning crescent?

It's the new moon tonight.

LANEY

Yeah, that's not –

D'NAY

And *this* is our professor who turns into a plant when the moon is hidden from the sky. During the new moon.

LANEY

Wait. *There are people who turn into plants!?*

KELTON

What, were you raised under a rock?

GRAYNE

Yes! Yes, that was more appropriate.

VEN2

Not really by choice. Some other times of the month maybe too; I'm not clear on the details.

D'NAY

So when Professor Jinks is in plant form, we learn in Plantae Lingua. Which is a language we learn in elementary school in this country, like I think you all learn Latin or something in the Boundary Territories.

LANEY

Ancient Greek, but.

KELTON

Whatever.
It's all Greek to me!

GRAYNE

Yes, yes!
There will literally never be a better time to use that line!

VEN2

Ignoring them

Okay. Crash course in Plantae Lingua: stand like so *(demonstrates)* and close your eyes.

LANEY

I didn't know that plants could–

GRAYNE

What, talk? Communicate? Have feelings? You are really insensitive.

KELTON

What, were you raised by wolves?

GRAYNE

"Raised by wolves!" Good one.

They slap hands or something that they do.

LANEY

I'm insensitive?

GRAYNE

God, half my friends are plants.

LANEY

Okay.

Fitzrow zooms through.

D'NAY

To Grayne and Kelton

Hey, Dynamic Duo: I feel like your inclusivity has become exclusive.

FITZROW

Extremes meet!

D'NAY

You know it, babe.

FITZROW

I'm trying to get to Hale's class, but it's totally not happening. Don't let 'em get ya down, Laney.

LANEY

Thanks, Fitzrow!

D'NAY

Be where you are.

FITZROW

You are so right.

Fitzrow is gone.

LANEY

Can I just – one thing at a time: why is Fitzrow always moving?

D'NAY

Oh, yeah, ze can zoom anywhere within a quarter mile, but can never choose the destination.

LANEY

That's – okay.

VEN2

Back to…

D'NAY

Yes.

VEN2

Your first experience with Plantae Lingua might be a little, uh….

LANEY

A little what?

VEN2

Well, sometimes people –

D'NAY

Best not to set up any expectations….

LANEY

Sometimes people what?

VEN2

Yeah okay. You're right.

D'NAY

You'll be fine. You are pretty evolved.

VEN2

Just stand like so.

They all do so.

D'NAY

Close your eyes.

VEN2

It might help if we hold hands.

BAM. Once VEN2 & D'NAY take Laney's hands, there is a cataclysmic shift. Lights, sound, atmosphere. Laney is catapulted into a different realm. The following Plantae Lingua sequence involves the entire company and is a psychedelic ritual rock concert performance art piece. It may include, but is not limited to: dance, ritual movement, pyrotechnics, shadow puppetry, light show, mask work, animation. Think Hedwig and the Angry Inch and Greek theatre meet psychedelic mushrooms.

It is otherworldly and strange.

Even stranger than that.

During the chanting section, Laney should feel like a fish out of water and will feel totally out of sorts. Please allow the actor to express zemself. Reactions may include, but are not limited to:
WHA?
WHAT IS GOING ON? What is going on? What is going on?
UH uhuhuhuhuhuh - can anyone else see this?
Have I tripped into some kind of psychedelic daymare?
This is like this is like this is like Little Shop of Horrors ate Alice in Wonderland and I don't know if I am here for it.
Is this real life?
What what what what what is happening?
Hello hello hello hello hello.

VOICES

THE EARTH THE SKY
THE SUN AND MOON
FARE THEE WELL
WE'LL BE BACK SOON

THE OCEAN, TREES,
THE ROOTED CLOUDS
THE CALLING WINDS
THEY WHISPER LOUD

THE LIFELONG FATES
LEFT UP TO CHANCE
THE EARTH, THE SKY
THE MOON AND PLANTS

MUSIC

IN THE BEGINNING THERE WERE PLANTS
AND THERE WAS WIND AND THERE WAS FIRE
AND THERE WERE OCEANS AND SKIES AND BEYOND
THEN THE PEOPLE CAME WITH PLANS
AND WITH THEIR EGOS AND DESIRES
AND SHRUNK THIS WONDROUS WORLD TO A TINY MONDE

AND THERE WAS MAGIC IN THE AIR
AND IN THE TRUNKS AND IN THE ROOTS
AND THE BROWN EARTH – IT WAS TRAMPLED
UNDER BLINDED BURNING BOOTS

AND THEY CUT ALL THE WISDOM DOWN
THEY BURNED ALL THE KNOWLEDGE TO THE GROUND

SO THEY SEVERED THE TIES
TO THE NATURE IN THEIR LIVES
AND THE WORLD SPLIT IN TWO IN THE FRAY
THERE WERE THE ONES WHO HAD IT ALL
AND THE ONES OUT OF CONTROL

THE MARGINALS ALL MOVE SIDEWAYS
THE MARGINALS ALL MOVE SIDEWAYS
THE MARGINALS ALL MOVE SIDEWAYS

It is the most outrageous thing Laney has ever experienced and ze lives in a world of magic.

Suddenly: back to the classroom. All are gone, but Laney, flanked by D'Nay and Ven2. Laney is out of sorts throughout the following.

Laney comes to.

LANEY

WHAT THE ACTUAL –

D'NAY

Oh good. We were getting worried.

VEN2

See I told you -

LANEY

WHAT WAS THAT!?!?!?

D'NAY

Okay. I told you Laney would come around. I'll leave you then. I gotta get to the forum on Students Against Everything and explain why they should be *for* something. (to Laney) You might wanna hydrate, take a little rest.

VEN2

Cool, see ya.

D'NAY

See ya, Ven.

LANEY

What?

VEN2

What what?

LANEY

Um, where's Ven?

VEN2

Yeah. Here.

LANEY

You're.

VEN2

Ven. Remember? Tried to get you to date our sex ed professor yesterday. It was awesome.

LANEY

But you–

VEN2

realizing

Oh, right! Yeah, this is my MA. I look different every day.

LANEY

You –
You look different every day.

VEN2

It sounds cool but it's a total drag. The shoe sizes alone. Plus, this is always happening.

LANEY

You're. Ven.

VEN2

Yeah, we met with Crux. I was going to tell you my MA, then we got sidetracked. Outside Bio.

LANEY

I thought you were just a really helpful stranger.

VEN2

Yeah. No.

LANEY

Wow. Last time I saw you, you were –

VEN2

Taller? Shorter? Fatter? Thinner? Lighter? Darker? Queerer? Straighter? More attractive? Less– c'mon, I'm always attractive though.

LANEY

You look different. Every day.

VEN2

That is the takeaway here. Yes.

LANEY

How do–
How does everyone know it's you?

VEN2

My charisma. Charm. Savoir faire?
Just kidding. I don't even know what that means.

LANEY

It's an ability to behave appropriately according to social situations.

VEN2

Oh. Okay. Then that.

We don't get many new students here. So I stand out. I guess. I mean, once the government allowed parents to genetically engineer their fetuses, who would choose us, right? Design your kid to have green eyes and perfect teeth and like, spin straw into gold. We are a dying breed, I guess.

LANEY

In my country we're not allowed to…

VEN2

To genetically engineer the unborn?

LANEY

Not so much.

VEN2

But you can use magic to change things though, right? Improve the way people live.

LANEY

Yeah. It's –

VEN2

Amazing.

LANEY

But the Boundary Territories are –

VEN2

A utopia I bet.

LANEY

It's nice, but I didn't belong there. I mean, the whole country is super small – it's a postage stamp compared to this place. Screw up once, you'll never live it down.

VEN2

Yeah, but you actually use magic for something meaningful - promote peace, reduce pollution, avoid all bad hair days.

LANEY

I guess. But not here?

VEN2

Not here. No. "No significant use of magic may be made in the government or execution thereof" blah blah blah. It's a list a mile long.

LANEY

I don't get it.

VEN2

Created by people who lived hundreds of years ago. In a different time. There wasn't indoor plumbing or flying cars or colonies on the moon or anything back then. Why the heck would you come here?

LANEY

Banished from utopia I guess. I mean– My family thought it'd be good for me to be around more Marginals. Here.

(Cont.)
That's why. I'm here. There isn't really a whole school dedicated to us back home.

VEN2

How's that working out?

LANEY

Honestly, you are all anything but marginal. Look at you.

VEN2

Awwww. You're not so marginal yourself.

LANEY

What do you think the professor meant by that: "The marginals all move sideways."

VEN2

Honestly? I only understand about 50% of what goes on in this class at any give time.

Laney lists a bit and drops a bunch of AA from zer bag.

Are you okay?

LANEY

I guess. I feel a little funny though.

VEN2

Yeah, probably should have warned you. The aftereffects of Plantae Lingua set in about 15 minutes after a session and they are sometimes…

LANEY

Are sometimes….?

VEN2

Sit. I'll get it.

LANEY

Are sometimes…?

Ven2 picks up AA.

VEN2

What is all this?

LANEY

Oh, it's nothing. It's called Art Abandonment. I create these little bookmarks with sayings and then drop them anonymously for people to find. People do it all over the world - pottery, crochet, paintings. I even saw someone making little dolls out of pipe cleaners. I'll zing you the info if you want.

VEN2

These are really cool. (reading) "Be who you are." "You have everything you need." Very ar-tis-tic. You are definitely not from here.

LANEY

I was gonna sneak this one into your bag.

VEN2

"Be the change."

LANEY

Which is retrospect seems...

VEN2

Prescient?

LANEY

referring to another bookmark

I guess. I made this one for Crux.

Crux pops in.

CRUX

You called?

LANEY

Hey.

CRUX

Oy, you don't look so good.

LANEY

I don't feel so good.

VEN2

Plantae Lingua.

CRUX

First time? First time's the worst. Ven and I were headed to grab some food on the way to D'Nay's "Do something" or "Stop doing nothing" or "Quit Cancelling" talk. I dunno. What's it called?

LANEY

Oh, okay. Ven was just --

CRUX

Oh, do you think THAT's Ven?

LANEY

Yeah, ze just explained.

CRUX

That's not Ven.

LANEY

Hold up.

CRUX

No, I'm totally screwing with you. It's Ven. Isn't it obvious?

VEN2

Very funny, Crux. /

LANEY

I feel funny.

CRUX

to Ven

/Oh, c'mon, mate, I'd know you anywhere.

VEN2

Yeah, I know. I know.

remembering the AA from Laney for Crux

I almost forgot, Laney made you this.

Gives it to Crux

CRUX

Awww.
(reading) "You are enough."
That's. *(stalled for a moment)*
Thanks, Laney.

LANEY

What if we could taste clouds?

CRUX

Uh oh. I know that look. Plantae Lingua hangover on the horizon. Let's take a detour to find somewhere calm for this little birdie to lie down. I have a feeling it's gonna be a wild ride.

They start to usher Laney out.

LANEY

I think my tongue is too big for my mouth.

CRUX

Okay, little frog. Okay.

LANEY

Ribbit. Ribbit. Ribbit.

Laney takes off abruptly in another direction.

CRUX

WHERE ARE YOU GOING?

VEN2

Mayday, mayday! Frog is going rogue!

LANEY

I don't know where I am going! Everything looks the same in this school! Will it be this way forever?!??!?!

CRUX

It's kinda like having a child.

VEN2

Awwww.

SCENE 5: The Room is Spinning

20 minutes later. Laney is on the floor, suffering the aftereffects of the Plantae Lingua experience. It is a strange trip. Crux, Ven2 and Kelton are attending to zer. They are in the art room, trying to manage Laney who has become a wandering drunken toddler. Crux and Ven2 are in the middle of a friendly, but heated discussion.

CRUX

To Ven

Oh please, the first time you did Plantae Lingua at this school you hugged every person you saw for the rest of the day and said "science is magic" about a hundred times. (to Laney) Try not to touch everything, Laney. You'll be fine.

VEN2

(to Crux) And you, –
(to Laney) Laney, climbing is a bad idea-
(to Kelton) Kelton, could I get some help here?

KELTON

On it.

VEN2

(to Crux) – you – wait, what did you do?

CRUX

Nothing. It didn't really affect me.

VEN2

No no! Now I remember. You laughed so hard you peed your pants. Then we stole new pants from the lost and found and you did it AGAIN. Twice. You peed your pants two times.

KELTON

(to Laney)

You don't have to pee, do you?

VEN2

(continuing to Crux)

No, wait! Three! Three times. Cause there was that other time –

CRUX

You cried at lunch and said the salad was depressed.

VEN2

It was. It was depressed.

Laney spins.

LANEY

The room is spinning.

CRUX

No, honey, you're spinning.

Laney goes down.

LANEY

It's like Christmas.

Laney tries to get up.

VEN2

It'll pass. Just stay down.

D'Nay finds them.

D'NAY

What the heck happened?

LANEY

D'NAY!!!!!!

CRUX

referring to Laney

This.

LANEY

D'Nay is like a firework. Boom. Boom. Boom.

CRUX

This happened.

D'NAY

When I left class everything was fine.

VEN2

It was Laney's first experience. Ever. Do you remember your first time?

KELTON

Plantae Lingua effects different people different ways.

LANEY

I have forgotten to water so many plants.

D'NAY

(responding to Crux)

Oh really? I didn't think it was that trippy this time.

LANEY

Do you think I'm a murdered.
Murdred.
Murderrrrer.
Why are words so hard!?

D'NAY

Uhhhhh.

KELTON

I got something that'll make you feel better. I can give you a sample – first one's on me.

Kelton tries to offer Laney pills that look suspiciously like mints.

LANEY

Oh, I thought you were mean, but maybe you're not.

Laney goes to accept.

KELTION

Wow. You just say whatever you think don't you.

Crux, Ven2 and D'Nay shut it down.

CRUX

No no no no.
Don't pull /that sh–

D'NAY

Oh, *hell* no. What are you –

VEN2

Kelton can make people 20% sleepier.

KELTON

Awww, what'd I ever do to you?

CRUX

Ze pawns mints off to newbies and then uses an MA to make it seem like they are on sedatives.

Scandalized.

LANEY

Oh my gosh, did you just offer me drugs?

KELTON

Technically no?

LANEY

clingy

Does this mean I belong?

Chartreuse enters.

CHARTREUSE
Yeah, you're not supposed to be in here.

D'NAY
Who died and left you in charge?

CHARTREUSE
Just saying.
Not that anyone ever comes into the *art* room anymore.
Or does actual art at this stupid excuse for an educational institution.

D'NAY
Why are you looking at me?

CHARTREUSE
To D'Nay

Project much?

Ya'll remember art, right?

VEN2
Laney here just experienced Plantae Lingua for the first time.

LANEY
Hi. I'm Laney. I just did a plant thing. *(Imitating plant)* Shhhhhhh Shhhhhhh Shhhhhh.

CHARTREUSE
Awwww, you're cute.

LANEY

I feel like a beached jellyfish./ Blub blub blub.

CHARTREUSE

You are really feeling it, huh.

LANEY

Did you know magic is real?

CHARTREUSE

Take that child to the nurse. I've never seen a reaction this severe.

VEN2

Ze'll be fine.

Laney is on the ground looking at Crux's feet.

LANEY

Omigod, Crux, I can totally see you hover from here.

CRUX

What! Who told you that.

Looking at D'Nay.

D'NAY

Oh come on. Why do you always think it is me.

CRUX

Because it is always you.

CHARTREUSE

looking at Laney's level, regarding Crux's hovering

Honestly, I've never seen it.

LANEY

To Chartreuse

You're like a snarky unicorn.

CHARTREUSE

Awwww, #goals. Enchanté. Je m'appelle Chartreuse.

LANEY

Like the color?

CHARTREUSE

So my Papa can turn anything orange and my Dad can turn anything purple so they thought it'd be fun to engineer me to be able to turn anything –

LANEY

chartreuse!

CHARTREUSE

Check out your underwear.

All look.

Disgruntled responses simultaneous to:

LANEY

WOW.
That is very
bright. I'm a rainbow bunny!

CRUX

Are you kidding me!
That is like the fourth
time you've done this to
me. I just got these.

CHARTREUSE

Don't get your panties in twist.

KELTON

regarding the pun

Excellent idiom use right there. Where's Grayne?!

LANEY

to Chartreuse

So your parents

CHARTREUSE

made me this way. Yeah. They thought I'd feel out of place if I wasn't like them. So they made me completely average like you losers.

D'NAY

Harsh, Char.

CHARTREUSE

Nothing says love like squelching someone's potential in utero.

LANEY

Is that why the school is so

CHARTREUSE	CRUX
ugly?	Hideous?

LANEY

Vibrant. I was going to say vibrant. Like a kaleidoscope.

VEN2

Festive, really. It's super festive.

Laney gives Chartreuse an AA.

LANEY

Oh I made this for you.

CHARTREUSE

reading

"You are allowed to be more than one thing." Honey, you just met me.

LANEY

I feel so many things.

CHARTREUSE

That's really sweet
or really creepy.

LANEY

Singing from the Plantae Lingua

"The Marginals all move sideways/ The Marginals -"

CHARTREUSE

What's that now?

CRUX

Where did you hear that?

VEN2

In Jinks' class today.

CRUX

That's weird.

LANEY

I thought it was weird too.
Why, why is that weird??

CRUX

Because I've been thinking that phrase all day.

CHARTREUSE

Okay. Hold up. Me too.

Through the following Laney becomes more manic.

LANEY

Ohmygosh I knew it meant something. I've been waiting for this this this this like beacon no this uh, sign, a sign, that we all can amount to more ya know like we are all cogs in the machine, but together we make the machine go. And I feel like– *bam*– the Plantae Lingua made it all clear. It was right here like RIGHT HERE can you touch it NO NO you can't because there's this veil see and WE we are on this side and the ANSWER is on that side and we just don't like REACH OUT and – we have to go SIDEWAYS see? "The Marginals all move SIDEWAYS" Wait. WAIT.–I have an idea and I'm going to sketch it out in a 47-part diagram.

D'NAY

Kelton, I hate to say this, but I think we need you to do something.

LANEY

Now, does anyone have PAPER? I'm sorry about the rainforests, D'Nay, but I need PAPER.

KELTON

Say no more.

Kelton gently touches Laney or makes a deliberate motion to make Laney 20% sleepier.

LANEY

Actually.

Laney is suddenly much more tired.

LANEY (cont)

I'm gonna *(lay down)*

Kelton does it again.
Laney is suddenly asleep.

D'NAY

Thanks, Kelton.

CRUX

It's for the best.

VEN2

What do you think the 47-part plan was?

All look to VEN2.

What?! Was no one else curious?

SCENE 6: Someone is Lying

The next morning. Outside the school. D'Nay, Trune, Laney, Ven3, Fitzrow, Crux are coming in for the school day one by one. They ultimately gather in a huddle to plan something big. D'Nay & Trune are onstage to start. Others straggle in.

D'NAY

Now we're organized. We got the platform. We got the people. I can't believe we figured this out overnight. I AM SO PUMPED I could -

TRUNE

Dance?

Ven3 & Laney enter.

D'NAY

Oh please. There's no time.

VEN3

I still think that Laney's 47-part plan from yesterday was strong up until point twenty-three.

Fitzrow enters.

LANEY

Very funny, Ven.

FITZROW

I got lost at point nine but solid effort, Laney.

D'NAY

(continuing from before)

"The Marginals all move sideways!" Why didn't I think of it before? The law states:

Crux enters.

TRUNE

-"no significant use of magic may be employed to change the government or the laws thereof" – (looking at D'Nay) What? I listen to you.

VEN3

But we are **in**significant!

CRUX

Well done, Ven. We are *totally* insignificant.

FITZROW

"The marginals all move sideways" – what a poetic interpretation of the path towards progress Laney.

LANEY

Oh, uh. Thank you.

D'NAY

We are gonna take this school out of the Dumpster Fire of Misery and into the Realm of Empowering Possibilities in which student government is Relevant and Being *For* Something Matters.

TRUNE

By ....?

D'NAY

We talked about this! Don't you read my zings?

TRUNE

Of course I read your –

D'NAY

By sharing our ten-point plan at this morning's assembly and demonstrating how even *marginal* abilities can coalesce to affect change.

TRUNE

Okay. Then we need to know what everyone can do.

D'NAY

What?

TRUNE

If we are going to share this manifesto or whatever with the whole school to galvanize the efforts of the masses and save the rainforests, we need to know everyone's MA.

All look to Laney.

LANEY

Oh, uh.

FITZROW
"There is no 'i' in team!"

D'NAY
Okay.
(*As in: reign it in, Fitzrow.*)

VEN3
I agree with Trune.

FITZROW
But there is in "individual." In fact there are 2 - no wait (*counting*) 3.

VEN3
C'mon. We all know and trust each other here, right? We got your back, Laney, whatever your MA is.

CRUX
Calm down, Ven. Laney will tell us when ze's ready.

VEN3
I just don't know what the big deal is. Ze is here because ze's like us. Why do you care so much?

D'NAY
It's not *that* important.

TRUNE
It kind of is. It's part of /who we

VEN3
It IS important. It's a deep-seated part of a person's identity.

CRUX

Is it really? What – we *are* our MAs now? It shouldn't matter what ze can –

VEN3

I just don't understand why –

CRUX

Some things are private, /people!

TRUNE

Nothing is private these days.

VEN3

Why do you even care so much?

CRUX

It's just - dude, let it be –/

LANEY

OKAY okay. I get it. You don't trust me cause you don't know my MA.

CRUX

You don't have to tell us if you aren't ready. God, Ven, you are so insensitive. Not everyone wants to be an open book.

VEN3

Well some of us can't help it!

LANEY

It's fine. It's fine.

CRUX

No it's not. Take a walk, Ven. Pushiness doesn't look good on you.

VEN3

Doesn't look good on me? That's low.

LANEY

Stop fighting! Please!
<A moment to gather resolve>
I can make people sneeze, okay?

A breath.

CRUX

Great.

D'NAY

Oh.
Okay.

VEN3

You can–

FITZROW

Brilliant.

D'NAY

Whoa. *(remembering)* Was that you in Bio?

VEN3

See? *(to Laney)* Thank you for sharing. *(Sneeze.)* Now we can all move past this *(sneeze)*-

LANEY

It's hilarious, isn't it?

D'NAY

It's not. Not hilarious. (sneeze)

TRUNE

Well, it's kind of– (sneeze)

D'NAY

What did I do? (sneeze)

CRUX

See, this is why – (sneeze)

VEN3

See, now we are all on the same (sneeze) page (sneeze)

All sneeze and fall silent.

LANEY

My whole family is extraordinary. My sister can change the weather, my brother talks to freakin' animals. My mother got a special dispensation to restore the polar ice caps and my father is reinforcing the ozone layer above the Boundary Territories. And I essentially give people allergies. I'm a waste. I'm pollen. I'm like human pollen.

Everyone sneezes.

VEN3

If you could– *(stop making us sneeze)*

TRUNE

Does anyone have a tissue?

Laney produces a box from zer bag.

LANEY

Hazard of the job.

TRUNE

Thanks.

VEN3

Yeah.

D'NAY

Thanks.

LANEY

I thought. I thought it'd be different here. But I see all of you. You are all so *extraordinary*. I mean. Even without your MAs. D'Nay, you single-handedly organized all this. Ven, you are funny and likable no matter your appearance. Crux, you are so cool and principled and honest. You are smart and funny and dedicated and kind. All of you. Just by being yourselves. I just. I wanted to feel like I was part of something. But I never fit. I never fit anywhere.

Silence.

CRUX

Check your pocket.

LANEY

What?

CRUX

L o o k
in your pocket.

LANEY

Why...
Why is there a potato in my pocket.

VEN3

Whoa. There's one in mine too.

TRUNE

Bizarre.

CRUX

That's what I can do.

ALL	VEN3
What?	Wait, what?

CRUX

I can make potatoes appear in people's pockets.

LANEY

But.

TRUNE

You can hover.

VEN3

Hold on.

FITZROW

I thought you could/ hover, dude.

VEN3

But you told us - you told me that you could hover. We've seen you hover./ I've seen it.

D'NAY

Honestly, I've never seen it.

CRUX

My family can FLY. *Fly*. My little sister. Can fly.

TRUNE

So you…

LANEY

Oh, Crux.

VEN3

You lied to me? To all of us.

FITZROW

checking pocket

Whoa. I got potato chips! And honestly, I was really hungry. Thank you, Crux.

VEN3

How could you? We trusted you. I trusted you.

CRUX

I – I don't know. It was easier to be extremely mediocre in a family of fly-ers than be the butt of a joke and not belong anywhere.

VEN3

That's BS.

D'NAY

C'mon, Ven.

VEN3

You let me believe that you had a different MA this whole time?! You know how hard it is for me to be like like like– this. What else haven't you told me?– (back 3 seconds) What are you keeping from me?– (back 3 seconds) Why don't you trust me?

D'NAY

There it is.

VEN3

to D'Nay, who has been messing with time

STOP DOING THAT!

CRUX

To Ven3

I do trust you. I just couldn't tell you.

VEN3

Whatever.

CRUX

There was never the right time. Things were always different.

VEN3

You mean, *I* was always different, don't you?

CRUX

No, I know you were always you. I know that. I just wasn't ready. I trust you; I just couldn't tell you.

VEN3

Yeah? Potato, potahto.

Drops potato on the floor and exits.

CRUX

Ven! C'mon, Ven!

Crux rushes after Ven.

Fitzrow has just finished eating the bag of chips.

FITZROW

Look, I know things are super tense right now, but, I gotta say, that was, hands down, the best bag of chips I've ever had.

LANEY

Oh, this is complicated.

D'NAY

Yeah it is.

LANEY

No, I mean, Ven has long-held romantic feelings for Crux, and was about to reveal them - but now feels wounded, a feeling exacerbated by a natural tendency to deflect using humor. And Crux has also always wanted to confide in Ven, but thought ze would think less of zer for lying in the first place. This is only further complicated by the fact that they are best friends and neither wants a romantic relationship to get in the way of their friendship but both are madly, deeply, irrevocably in love with each other.

TRUNE

Whoa. How do you know all that?

GRAYNE & KELTON wander in.

LANEY

I can read minds.

ALL

WHAT???

LANEY

For the love of – If I could read minds, would I seriously be at this school?! (referring to Ven/Crux relationship) Anyone can see that. Can't you all see that.

FITZROW

Laney, dude, I think you are on a different emotional wavelength than we are.

D'NAY

Yeah I did not pick up on that.

TRUNE

I'd rather go to the dentist than talk about my feelings.

KELTON

Me too.

GRAYNE

Me three.

D'NAY

Where'd you two come from?

GRAYNE

We were invisible.

LANEY

You can become – !?!

KELTON

If we could be invisible, do you think–

LANEY

Okay okay. I get it.

GRAYNE

It's a feeling. Metaphorical invisibility.

KELTON

I thought you were all emotionally leveled up and stuff.

LANEY

I get it. I get it.

GRAYNE

We came to get you. Something weird is happening.

D'NAY

What's happening?

GRAYNE & KELTON

It's the plants.

SCENE 7: Farcical Hoard Chase Sequence

The group of students run the seemingly never-ending halls of the school to find the plants. This can be accomplished in a variety of ways and is an opportunity to include the larger ensemble in an ode to the quintessential chase sequence.

Here is an offering: three parts of chaos scored to wild music. It probably needs to be three beats, whatever you do.

1. Perhaps the first is all out mayhem.
2. Perhaps the second flips to "Chariots of Fire" slow motion.
3. Maybe the third is back to craziness.

Whatever you discover as an ensemble, let it be fun, funny, and team-oriented, something in direct contrast to the tenderness that is about to come in Scene 8. Vocalizations are welcome and encouraged.

SCENE 8: Jet Lag

Inside. The next moment. All run by the room where Ven is to see what is going on with the plants. Laney pokes in to talk to Ven.

LANEY

Ven, hey. (calling to others) I'll be right there. (to Ven) Where's Crux?

VEN3

Potato farming I guess.

LANEY

Come on.

Are you okay?

VEN

I don't wanna talk about it.

LANEY

Alright.

Look, I'm sorry I didn't tell you sooner. You and Crux and D'Nay and everyone have been so good to me. Well, not Grayne. Grayne has been miserable, but even Kelton tried to offer me drugs, ya know. Which seems like an effort.

VEN3

It's not you I'm upset about.

LANEY

It's hard to be completely embarrassed by what you're capable of.

VEN3

referring to Ven's own appearance

You don't think *this* is embarrassing?

LANEY

The way I feel about my MA does not invalidate the way you feel about yours.

VEN3

Seriously, you should be a therapist.

LANEY

You are not the first person who has said that to me. Today.

VEN3

How could ze? *(referring to CRUX)* I just don't get it – we tell each other everything. We're best friends. I feel so –

LANEY

Betrayed, listless, unmoored.

VEN3

If I don't know Crux, I feel like...like.... I don't know myself.

LANEY

Before I came here, I didn't have a clue who I was. I felt like a different person every day.

VEN3

Ha ha.

LANEY

I read this book once where they said that we get jet lag because when we travel really fast- by plane or rocket or flying car or whatever - that we leave our souls behind. And they need time to catch up. That's how I've always felt. Like if I could just slot everything into place, I'd be a person, but it's like - like the parts of myself are those opposable magnets and they keep pushing each other away. But here. Well. It's the first time I felt like everything fell into place. Like, the magnets turned around, and suddenly I'm a whole being.

VEN3

I'm not sure what that has to do with anything.

LANEY

We're all just doing our best. Just trying to slot into place.

You know who you are. You're just out of sync for a moment.

You and Crux are magnets. Right now maybe you are just facing the wrong directions.

VEN3

(Sneeze)

LANEY

Gesundheit.

VEN3

'Scuse me.

LANEY

Bless you.

VEN3

Must be allergies.

LANEY

Yeah, we don't get those back home.

VEN3

Lucky. *(sneeze)* Wait, are you using your–

LANEY

I'm not –

VEN3

Let me *(sneeze)* get a *(sneeze)*

Ven3 drops below a table or behind closet door to get a tissue while sneezing. Ven2 (Ven from the Plantae Lingua scene) emerges. As the Vens switch around in this and the subsequent scenes, they are all wearing what Ven3 wore, in the same size. It may end up being oversized or way too small. Embrace it.

VEN2

It's really not (sneeze)–

LANEY

Ven.

VEN2

Yes.

LANEY

You are – you're different. You –

VEN2

Ha ha./ *(to Ven's next line)*

LANEY

You were -/ *(to Laney's next line)*

VEN2

/Every day I look–

LANEY

–this is how you looked yesterday.

VEN2

Now I know you are joking. Cause that *never* happens.

LANEY

No – you –

VEN2

Joke's on you. I'm like stepping into a river – I'm never the same person twice.

LANEY

LookLookLOOK! *(Forcing Ven2 to see)*

VEN2

I – What?!

LANEY

Look, I think there's a mirror somewhere over–

Laney guides Ven2 to a mirror that is conveniently located behind a desk/door/locker. Make magic happen however you need to!

VEN2

Off

What on earth

Ven (from the first scene) emerges.

VEN

continued seamlessly

–is going on?!!!

LANEY

You - You changed again!

VEN

I– *(looking down)* oh, come on!

LANEY

Something weird is happening.

VEN

Honestly, it always feels like something weird is happening.

LANEY

Let's find the others.

Laney exits in the wrong direction then returns.

That is not the right way. I will never figure out the layout of this school!

VEN

Oh this *(pants/dress/whatever Ven is wearing)* is really uncomfortable! Why did I wear this today?!

They run out together.

SCENE 9: What am I looking at?

The art room. Grayne, Kelton, D'Nay, Fitzrow and Trune have just arrived. Grayne is overwhelmed by smells in the scene; Grayne's MA is: can smell big emotions. They are taking in the scene: a lot of potted plants - Professor Jinks plus a bunch more.

Chartreuse is doing art.

There are a lot of plants.

More than that.

D'NAY

Taking in foliage

What am I looking at?

FITZROW

I like that they added more nature to this place. Feels very relaxing.

CHARTREUSE

So the prodigal children return home.

FITZROW

Looking at Chartreuse's art

Chartreuse, what psychedelic artwork, brah.

CHARTREUSE

Don't worry. I don't expect you all to actually create anything.

Chartreuse continues to do art, unfazed.

TRUNE

(to Professor Jinks the plant)

Hey professor.

GRAYNE

To all

You know how Professor Jinks turns into a plant every new moon?

TRUNE

Wait a second…– *(calculating)*

GRAYNE

Yeah, it's not the new moon anymore.

D'NAY

So….

FITROW

So Professor Jinks never changed back into a a a… professor?

D'NAY

Okay.
And.
Wait. *(taking in other plants)*
What about all this?

KELTON

gesturing to a plant

That's Hale.

D'NAY

Professor Hale.

TRUNE

to the plant

Hey Professor Hale.

D'NAY

Okay. That's.

TRUNE

approaches Hale

Sorry about that paper. I'd give you some excuse, but I know you value honesty: I procrastinated until the last minute and then I really enjoyed the writing process and want to make it something I'm proud of and something worth reading. I'll get it in to you tomorrow.

D'NAY

What about –-

FITZROW

This is a lot of greenery.

VEN and Laney rush in to join the others.

TRUNE

gesturing to another plant

Then who is this?

VEN

recognizing Crux as a plant at once

CRUX!

LANEY

Why are there so many *(plants)* –
Chartreuse, are you practicing still life or something?

VEN

Oh my god, what happened? Crux!

TRUNE

But it's not just/ –

D'NAY

This is like half the school.

FITZROW

These are all people?! Wicked.

D'NAY

Why did half of the school turn into plants??!!!

FITZROW

And not wicked in a good way wicked. Wicked like *wicked* wicked.

D'NAY

In the art room.

GRAYNE

I think… I think they're all hopeless.

LANEY

What?

GRAYNE

I can – I mean, my MA is… I can smell big emotions.

LANEY

Oh, that's interesting. Is that why you're so prickly?

KELTON

You just get right to it, don't you.

LANEY

I don't think it's a secret.

GRAYNE

responding to Laney

I mean, I guess. I never thought of it that way. It is a lot to handle.

KELTON

We were talking to Jinks and then we realized that normally there aren't any plants in here. And when Crux ran by all upset, that was it. Boom, Crux turned into a plant. So we dragged zer in. And when we started to look closer –

FITZROW

I think that philodendron's in my Calc class.

KELTON

To Ven

What happened between you and Crux?

LANEY

Uuuuhh

VEN

Oh no. It's my fault. I was awful. Crux, I'm so sorry!

D'NAY

What the hell are we gonna do with all this...foliage? We have to change them back.

Blip in time. Time abruptly jumps back to 15 minutes ago. We are back to the fight between Ven3 and Crux.

VEN3

But you told us - you told me that you could hover. We've seen you hover./ I've seen it.

D'NAY

Honestly, I've never seen it.

CRUX

My family can FLY. *Fly*. My little sister. Can fly.

TRUNE

So you...

DELANEY

Oh, Crux.

VEN3

You lied to me? To all of us.

FITZROW

checking pocket

Whoa. I got potato chips! And honestly, I was really hungry. Thank you, Crux.

VEN3

How could you? We trusted you. I trusted you.

Time speeds forward to now and repeats exactly, but Kelton has now changed into a plant and Ven is different.

LANEY

Uuuuhh

VEN3

Oh no. It's my fault. I was awful. Crux, I'm so sorry!

D'NAY

What the hell are we gonna do with all this…foliage? We have to change them – WAIT.

TRUNE

Didn't this already happen?

FITZROW

Wicked. I thought you could only go back and forth 3 seconds, D'Nay!

D'NAY

I *can* only go back and forth 3—-

LANEY

Noticing present-moment Ven has changed again to Ven3

VEN!

GRAYNE

Everything smells really confusing. Wait, where's Kelton?

Time abruptly jumps back to the post-Plantae Lingua exchange. Exactly as before:

CRUX

That's not Ven.

LANEY

Hold up.

CRUX

No, I'm totally screwing with you. It's Ven.
Isn't it obvious?

VEN2

Very funny, Crux. /

LANEY

I feel funny.

CRUX

/Oh, c'mon, mate, I'd know you anywhere.

Abruptly back to the present.

GRAYNE has also transformed into a plant.

Now with Ven2:

D'NAY

What the hell are we gonna do with all this…foliage? We have to change them – WAIT.

TRUNE

Didn't this already happen?

FITZROW

Wicked.

LANEY

Ven.

VEN2

Yes.

ALL

Whoa.

TRUNE

to D'Nay

Are you doing this?

D'NAY

I can't do this. *Can I do this?!*

VEN2

Where's Grayne?

Time Travel flips back to Laney's first day.

CRUX

So don't like divulge what someone else can do. It's rude.

VEN

But you can share *your MA* if you want.

LANEY

My –

VEN

You know, your MA, your *Magical Ability.*

CRUX

Pressuring others to divulge their MAs, also: not cool.

VEN

What?

CRUX

Oh please.

VEN

I wasn't doing anything of the sort. Besides, I'm an open book. I'm happy to share what I can do.

CRUX

Laney's not interested.

LANEY

I'm kinda interested.

VEN

See.

CRUX

Plenty of time for you to talk about yourself later, Ven. Right now, I have to get Laney to class. Ze's new. Obviously. I'm showing zer around.

VEN

Of course. Welcome, Laney, welcome. As you can see, we are vaguely disgruntled, moderately disillusioned, and completely average here. Congratulations on your enrollment.

Abruptly back to present with VEN.
Trune & Fitzrow have also become plants.

D'NAY

I can't do this. *Can I do this?!*

VEN

Where's Grayne?

LANEY

And Trune? And –

D'NAY

Trune! And Fitzrow. Fitz!

VEN

They are all

D'NAY

PLANTS!

LANEY

Oh no. This is –

VEN

We gotta –

LANEY

Oh no ohnoohnoohnoohno.

D'NAY

What do we do?

LANEY

This is all my fault. I'm so sorry.

Laney runs out of the art room.

VEN

Laney, wait!

D'NAY

What the hell is going on?

CHARTREUSE

Still doing art

Nature, baby. Nature is reclaiming its due.

D'NAY

Why aren't you freaking out?

CHARTREUSE

It's just another day that ends in Y in Magicville, baby.

VEN

Chartreuse, practically the entire school has has has become vegetables.

CHARTREUSE

So the million dollar question is: why are *we* still here?

D'NAY

Why *are* we still here?
I'm going to get Laney.

D'NAY runs off.

CHARTREUSE

This is the most action the art room has seen in years.
Maybe I'll paint me a biiiiig still life.

SCENE10: All the Feels

Laney is beating zerself up/weeping/upset in the bathroom/ hallway/somewhere else.

D'NAY

Mind if I come in?

LANEY

Oh hey.

D'NAY

Why um
Why do you think this is your fault?

LANEY

Oh uh

D'NAY

Cause if you have any ideas about how to get everyone back - I don't really have a green thumb, so.

LANEY

I – okay
I
Please don't hate me.
At my old school -
I told Ven that I came here because my family wanted me to be around more Marginals. But I
I was kicked out – well, okay, *asked to leave* my old school because I apparently
Madepeoplefeeltoomuch

D'NAY

Come again?

LANEY

I
I make people feel too much.

D'NAY

Is that
Like
Some kind of secondary MA?

LANEY

No, I don't know. That's just it. I was just
Just being myself. I can really only make people sneeze but something about having me around made other people go a little um haywire. And once the school figured out it was me, they uh, strongly suggested I find another educational institution.

D'NAY

Okay.

LANEY

You hate me now. No one wants to feel anything these days. I guess. I don't know how it happens. I'm just me.

D'NAY

Well. You do tend to just say what you feel.

LANEY

Yeah and what's wrong with that?

D'NAY

Nothing. It's great. I wish more people would be like that.

LANEY

So that's my grave offense? I say what I feel and I make stupid bookmarks. I'm a real renegade, right?

D'NAY

Wait.
Yeah. You do.
It's like your secret MA.

LANEY

My secret –

D'NAY

Not a real magical ability, but like a little secret one.
Your little bookmarks –

D'NAY removes the bookmark Laney made from earlier: "be your own art."

(cont)
I have been carrying this bookmark around since
Since you gave it to me. "Be your own art." And you know what I actually did last night?
I danced.
I danced for the first time in years.

LANEY

That's cool.

D'NAY

It is. I mean, I gave up dance to run student government. Everyone gave up something when we were told to focus on more "worthwhile pursuits." And honestly? I haven't felt like myself since I gave it up.
You did that.
You reminded me. About how I loved it. And I thought: *why not?*

LANEY

Wait. What if– What if we all have a secret MA?

D'NAY

What?

LANEY

You just said it. What if we all have a kind of secret – *(figuring something out)*

Chartreuse is doing art, right? That's ALL Chartreuse does: art.

D'NAY

Yeah so?

LANEY

We gotta go find Ven and Chartreuse right now. Come on.

Laney starts to pull D'Nay off.
Before they get out the door, they run into Ven2.

VEN2

Hey, I was just coming to find you two.

LANEY

What are you doing that is artistic?

VEN2

Um what?

LANEY

You - do you I dunno sculpt or like yodel or make papier-mâché masks or something?

VEN2

I – how – ??
I just picked up my guitar this week. I stopped playing last year, but earlier this week your little bookmark thinger fell outta my bag and –

LANEY

"Be the change."

VEN2

I used to write music. I wanted to be one of those singer-songwriters who spoke about the truth you know? Who rallied crowds in peaceful protest. So I I picked it back up….

D'NAY

to Laney

How did you know –

LANEY

I think I know how to un-pot those plants.

D'NAY

Not sure that's exactly the phrase, but okay.

LANEY

Let's go!

Laney goes boldly in the wrong direction again. Returns.

That is not the way. It looks like the way, but it is not, cause everything in this school looks the same.

My enthusiasm will not be blunted!

This is the way!
Let's go.

All three run off back to the art room.

SCENE 11: Time to Grow

Several hours later. The art room. It is transformed into a magical artistic wonderland. VEN has a guitar. Use whichever Ven can play the guitar for this scene. Oh, right: one of the Vens needs to play the guitar like a heartbreaking singer-songwriter troubadour from Shakespearean times. Cast that person.

LANEY

Are you almost ready? It's getting late and we don't want them to stay in herbal form too long. Who knows what it'll do to them?

VEN

All good here.

CHARTREUSE

Evaluating the artwork

I think my work here is done.

D'NAY

Did you put all of your bookmarks in their soil?

LANEY

Sticking the last ones in like plant markers

Yep yep. I got "wake up" for Kelton, "remember who you are" for Trune, "age is just a number" for Professor Hale, "You are the calm you seek," for Grayne, and "slow down" for Fitzrow.

VEN

What about Crux.

LANEY

I left that up to you.

Laney hands Ven a blank bookmark.

VEN

What I feel for Crux doesn't fit on a bookmark.

LANEY

Maybe that's where you start.

VEN writes the most beautiful,
touching, loving thing
that has has ever been written
from one friend to another
on the bookmark.

LANEY (cont.)

Perfect.

LANEY

D'Nay, are you ready?

D'NAY

I was born ready.

LANEY

Okay.
I'm gonna hit the lights!
Chartreuse, let's go.

Laney dims the lights.
Candles illuminate the space.
It is beyond an artistic wonderland.
Maybe the art glows.
It is magical: fairy lights, wonder, and possibility -
it is inside the mind of a child kind of magic.

Ven begins to pluck the guitar.
It is the most gorgeous melody:
simple but increasingly yearning.

During the music, D'Nay starts to dance.
The dance and song manifest the years of emotion
they have all held just beneath the surface.
It is rebellious and sad, joyful and plaintive,
angry and beautiful.

During the dance, the plants magically
return to human form, save Jinks.

When the dance ends, they are all all a little bit dirty
but transformed in more ways that one.

They all wonder and check in with each other.
Murmuring etc.

D'Nay runs to Fitzrow and throws arms around Fitz.

D'NAY

Fitz!

FITZROW

BABE!

D'NAY

You're back! Trune!

Trune runs to join them in a hug.

KELTON

That was the best rest I've ever had.

GRAYNE

Honestly, didn't mind it. Kinda nice to feel a little more grounded, ya know.

HALE

I feel older. *(hopeful)* Have I aged?!

KELTON

You still look 17 to me professor.

GRAYNE

I dunno. I think you could pass for 21 now.

FITZROW

21. That's a major win, right Professor Hale?

HALE

Major win, Fitzrow. Major win.

Ven runs to Crux.

VEN

Crux, I'm so sorry. Are you okay?

CRUX

I'm sorry. I'm sorry I didn't tell you sooner. I was…I was ashamed. How could you like someone who who

VEN

Who can give me French fries any time I want?

CRUX

Very funny.

VEN

Do you think I care about your stupid MA? Do you really think that's who you are?

CRUX

I – I don't know who I am

VEN

I'd recognize you anywhere, mate.

CRUX

Ha ha.

D'NAY

To Laney

How did you know that would work?

LANEY

Honestly, I didn't.

CHARTREUSE

I did. Have you seen the lame vacuum of feeling and expression this place has become since they abandoned all the arts at this bizarro school. It's no wonder we didn't turn into stone or accountants or house plants before this.

LANEY

But that's what art is isn't it? It's a risk. The risk of expressing who you really are. And that's what we did.

FITZROW

Looks like Professor Jinks is still a plant though. Bad luck, Professor dude.

KELTON

Consulting Jinks

It turns out, Professor Jinks actually prefers being a plant. Ze says it's a constant reminder of original magic.

TRUNE

(to Jinks)

Professor, I'm sorry about that project. I'll get it to you tomorrow. I'd give you some lame excuse, but honestly, I was turned into a house plant all day.

VEN

(to Crux)

Hey Crux, you wanna dance?

CRUX

Me?

CHARTREUSE

Best idea I've heard all day. Professor Jinks, could you provide us with some Plantae Lingua tunes? Laney, will you do me the honor?

LANEY

Totally.

CRUX

I – I can't actually –

VEN

What? Dance?

CRUX

Yeah, I cannot dance. And I feel –

LANEY

What – what do you feel?

CRUX

Uh, I dunno. Totally discombobulated? Terrified? Excited?

LANEY

Me too!

GRAYNE

Me three!

TRUNE

Me four!

VEN

Okay.
Let's dance anyway.

They do. Music thumps, lights go crazy. A la the end of a Shakespeare play, all dance. Throughout the following and with the magic of theatre, each Ven dances with Crux at some point. It is expressive, exuberantly joyful and fun for everyone.

END OF PLAY

Above: Kelton, D'Nay, Ven 2; 📷: Lou Liguori

www.ingramcontent.com/pod-product-compliance
Lightning Source LLC
LaVergne TN
LVHW091008080826
845145LV00003B/1178

* 9 7 8 1 9 6 6 0 0 4 1 3 4 *